History Is for the Birds

Bonnie Barb Frick

History Is for the Birds

by
Bonnie Barb Frick

ISBN-13: 978-1720317043
ISBN-10: 1720317046

Printed in the United States of America
by
CreateSpace, an Amazon.com Company

Available from Amazon.com and other retail outlets

DEDICATION

To those who serve

ACKNOWLEDGMENTS

Lancaster Downtown Walking Tour
Guides and Authors

HISTORY IS FOR THE BIRDS

CONTENTS

Chip and Chirp, Mourning Dove Friends   9

Lancaster, PA   11

Washington, D.C.   19

CHIP AND CHIRP,
MOURNING DOVE FRIENDS

Chip and Chirp, Mourning Dove friends,
enjoyed historical stories.
During three summer staycations,
they found not one boring.

Chip, the male of The Two,
led the discussions.
Chirp, the female of The Two,
injected pertinent questions.

They'd sit on a birdbath's edge,
dipping their tails within.
They'd sit in an old oak tree,
watching neighborhood kids.

Noticing a boy focused on a puddle,
they watched him with a chuckle.
He jumped into the puddle's center,
wondering if he'd be in trouble.

Chip and Chirp heard a nearby door
then saw a barefoot boy
licking a dripping ice cream cone,
bringing him moments of joy.

While sitting in the old oak tree,
The Two became distressed
when seeing a Blue Jay trying to steal
eggs from a sparrow's nest.

Chirp asked Chip what to do.
Frowning, Chip unsure,
knowing Blue Jays as fighters,
he couldn't reassure.

Chirp told Chip they must try
to save the sparrow's eggs.
She decided to deter that bird,
determined not to beg.

Chip got the message, made a plan
to chase the Jay away.
Taking turns diving at him,
they might dissaude the Jay.

For years to come, Chip and Chirp
spent summer days together
enjoying historical sites and tales,
no matter what the weather.

LANCASTER, PA

Flying fast and bullet straight,
nearing fifty-five,
gentle doves' soft coos,
soothing lullabies.

Avoiding swamps and thick forests,
preferring open living,
inhabiting suburbs and cities,
continually eating and drinking.

After surviving the first year,
they aim for four or five,
staying home, not migrating,
keeping a partner beside.

Being together on wires or limbs
or standing on the ground,
if one were forced to leave their place,
another'd come around.

Sometimes The Two could be found
sitting on courthouse steps.
Chip and Chirp, Mourning Dove friends,
chose stories to share next.

Historic Lancaster, Pennsylvania,
was home and playground, too;
another story for another day
at their private school.

James Hamilton designed this city
affecting both state and nation.
The Declaration of Independence,
a courthouse sensation.

For one day one year later
in this American nation,
the city served as federal capital,
building patriotism.

The Soldiers and Sailors Monument,
up at least four stories,
supported four male statues
honoring military glory.

Fulton Opera House on Prince
with 1500 seats,
the largest building of its kind.
It honored Robert's feats.

Chip nodded toward Central Market,
another Lancaster first–
the oldest publicly owned market
still in operation and first.

A tall building, their next site,
The Two began to fly
to the second highest building,
W.W. Griest so high.

Topping it, they couldn't believe
being fourteen stories above earth,
standing atop the first skyscraper
between Philly and Pittsburgh.

The Marriott and County Convention Center,
the tallest building in town,
at nineteen stories above the square
prompted the doves to stay down.

Another day, another story–
again, Chirp, the seeker.
Finding Chip atop the monument,
they flew to the Newspaper Reader.

Honoring the Steinman Brothers,
this realistic gent
sat quietly reading newspapers
too hard for The Two to bend.

Next, they flew to Steinman Hardware
to see the stained glass window
including a Conestoga wagon
above the doorway lintel.

Locally made Conestoga wagons,
an important commodity,
large, strong, built for rough roads,
sold within the city.

Another first for Lancaster–
Philadelphia and Lancaster Turnpike,
the first long-distance toll road built
in the states united.

Milton Hershey spent several years
in Lancaster City.
He opened a caramel candy company
before moving to Hershey.

A trip to Southern Market that day
to see Chip's rooftop residence
near the home of Jasper Yeates,
a prominent lawyer and justice.

That same day, The Two followed
a Historic Tour Guide,
learning about Montgomery House—
its curved back inside

Lancaster County Convention Center
near Thaddeus Stevens' cistern.
He, an Underground Railroad helper
and abolitionist.

The Guide pointed toward Swan Tavern
farther down Queen Street.
The first story, a local tavern;
the second, a hospital suite.

With the approaching end of June,
thoughts of red, white, and blue.
Time for celebrating the Fourth,
Chip searched for Chirp without clues.

After flying around and around,
Chip found Chirp atop
a narrow house on Church Street,
not far from his rooftop.

Built by men of competing businesses,
Ten-hour houses were plain.
C. Emlen Urban, outstanding architect,
did not design the same.

Among Urban's multitudinous kinds
of architectural designs–
churches, houses, schools, businesses
making Lancaster refined.

Deciding to study one more site,
Chip and Chirp looked
at Demuth Tobacco Shop
with no customers afoot.

Probably the oldest tobacco shop
in America to dwell;
Demuth's established in 1770
closed in 2012.

Philadelphia, Pittsburgh, then Lancaster,
Pennsylvania's third city.
Chip and Chirp spent several weeks
discussing Buchanan, a pity.

James Buchanan, the one President
from Lancaster's home state.
His presidency considered being the worst.
This President without a mate

Served in the War of 1812;
served as State Rep.,
U.S. Rep. and Senator,
Foreign Minister.

Departing, Chip and Chirp wondered
if President Buchanan's losing
Anne Coleman, the love of his life,
had affected his rulings.

Now August, time for Chip and Chirp
to end their historical tours,
discussed on this sightseeing day
Woolworth's five-story store.

Built on Queen by Architect
C. Emlen Urban,
a building topped with gold-toned towers
plus a rooftop garden.

He opened his first successful store
in 1899.
By the '70s, thousands of stores
had opened by this time.

The stores are gone, but his ideas
for selling products live on.
Time progresses, change continues;
time for The Two to fly on.

Chip requested they fly to Lancaster
County Courthouse on King.
Chip wasn't sure what had happened;
Chirp was a different being.

Chip found it hard to imagine their summer
visits nearing their end.
Chirp found their waning vacation time
made her feel abandoned.

As twilight appeared, Chip and Chirp
sat on the courthouse steps.
As the sun set this last day,
droplets dotted the steps.

Flying high, low, around,
Chip and Chirp, good friends,
slowly flew through a passing shower,
parting at summer's end.

WASHINGTON, D.C.

Virtually flying from Lancaster, PA,
to Washington, D.C.,
Chip and Chirp studied First Ladies–
Eleanor to Laura 43.

Chip was a dove, a Mourning Dove,
waiting behind the church;
another summer of sightseeing near
with his best friend Chirp.

Waiting behind Holy Trinity Church
for Chirp to arrive this summer,
he felt a little different inside,
okay, but somewhat glummer.

Holy Trinity Church's backyard
became a precaution
for Chip to forage for food and drink
under the nearby faucet.

Flying up Duke toward the church,
Chirp watched Chip look.
Landing beside him in the yard,
she saw a water-soaked book.

Able to read only part of the title:
TOGETHER. MODERN. LADY.
Ever inquisitive, yearning to learn,
they tugged the soaked book slowly

to the edge of the Church driveway,
then under a nearby bush.
Forty-one or Forty-three?
Silent, Chip smiled and pushed.

The summer adventure had started well.
The Two had a mystery to solve.
Using the soaked book as their source,
First Lady ventures evolved.

Suggesting they use the church as base
instead of Center City,
Chip wanted to learn about the church.
So, first, they studied Trinity.

One of Lancaster's oldest churches,
founded in 1730.
Matthew, Mark, Luke, John,
statues now clean, not dirty.

Old, wooden, exposed to weather,
the originals replaced by copies.
Matthew, Mark, Luke, John
now stood inside the lobby.

Chirp arrived with the rising sun
filled with anticipation,
eager to express her suggestion to talk
about the Constitution.

Article II, Section 1,
of the Constitution
names the President Commander-in-Chief,
lists his powers in the nation,

powers given by Senate consent.
First Ladies neglected–
stating nothing about their position
or duties therefore connected.

Serving as White House Hostess, but
receiving no money for life,
First Ladyship, an unofficial position,
filled by the President's wife.

> *"Chirp, what do you think about
> the unofficial position?"*

> *"Chip, I think the Founders forgot
> to consider a wife's contribution."*

Born in 1884,
Anna Eleanor Roosevelt
eventually married a distant cousin,
Franklin Delano Roosevelt.

Her father part of New York's gentry,
among the oldest and wealthiest.
Her mother, a Livingston Family descendant,
politically among the healthiest.

Father and mother physically attractive,
their daughter plain and shy.
Mother nicknamed her daughter Granny,
taught her manners to get by.

Married to Franklin in '05,
they moved next door to Mother,
controller of the family fortune
and her son moreover.

During her years as First Lady,
she served as White House Hostess.
Finding receptions somewhat boring,
she hosted them for promotion.

Not allowing the Secret Service
to accompany her;
they suggested she buy a pistol,
carry it–a trained amateur.

First Lady Roosevelt, advocate
for poor, women, minorities;
supported racial equality–
an independent First Lady.

A statement made by a person who considered
herself plain, shy, and not particularly happy to
become the First Lady of the United States,
First Lady Eleanor Roosevelt said: *Courage is
more exhilarating than fear and in the long run
it is easier. We don't have to become heroes
overnight. Just a step at a time, meeting each
thing that comes up, seeing it not as dreadful
as it appeared, discovering we have the strength
to stare it down.*

> "*Eleanor Roosevelt really changed
> the role of First Lady.*"

> "*Not allowing the Secret Service
> accompany her lacked safety.*"

Several mornings later, The Two
met at Holy Trinity.
Tugging their book from under the bush,
slowly, bird beaks gritting.

Born in 1885,
Elizabeth Virginia Wallace
married Harry S. Truman,
moved to Independence.

Her father, Deputy Surveyor of Customs,
known in the community.
Her mother from a wealthy family
nicknamed her daughter Bessie.

Depression followed bad finances;
he joined the alcohol scene.
Her father committed suicide
when Bess was only eighteen.

Emotional problems related to the death
of her failing father
reversed the roles of daughter and mother,
becoming a lifelong collar.

As White House Hostess, the First Lady
fulfilled social commitments.
She had no say in menu selections
with Roosevelt's former domestic.

President Truman complained to Bess
about brussel sprouts.
She told that domestic of the White House,
"Stop serving brussel sprouts!"

The same detested vegetable served
three consecutive evenings.
Soon after Mrs. Truman returned,
the domestic announced her leaving.

Speaking publicly about issues of concern,
absent from her purview.
The President considered her his adviser,
her opinions–good in his view.

First Lady Bess Truman said: *We are not any of us
happy to be where we are, but there's nothing to
be done about it except to do our best–and forget
about sacrifices and many unpleasant things that
bob up.*

> *"Following Mrs. Roosevelt
> as First Lady . . ."*

> *". . . another difficult task for Truman
> with problems since a baby."*

Flying along toward Holy Trinity,
Chip saw Chirp ahead.
He called to her to follow the leader;
she did with a tilt of her head.

Chip led Chirp to the top of the church,
then made a quick left turn,
following Duke, heading south,
before their return.

Born in 1896,
Mary Geneva Doud.
Not called Mary by family and friends,
Mamie served her proud.

Mamie's father, a meatpacker,
retired in his thirties.
Her sister's respiratory problems,
forced their changing cities.

While seeing friends during vacation,
Mamie met Dwight.
To her he was the spiffiest man;
he saw her–saucy and right.

After a brief engagement, they married
with 33 homes ahead.
Eisenhower taught his wife
to sew with needle and thread.

His quick and frequent promotions
brought protests from Mamie.
He explained his country's always first–
Mamie second to the Army.

Following the General's military career,
he ran for the Presidency.
Bess enjoyed being White House Hostess
and serving as First Lady.

Improvements in commercial air travel
enabled the Eisenhowers
to entertain more heads of state
and host foreign leaders.

The First Lady used intellect
to promote her husband's interests.
After two terms as President,
they purchased a private residence.

When asked what qualities she found necessary as
First Lady, she said: *Every President and First
Lady is an actor or actress. Nobody is simply
himself. It isn't possible, especially in public life.*

"Many promotions, many moves,
being second to the Army . . ."

". . . did not deter Mrs. Eisenhower
from enjoying being First Lady."

In the middle of Trinity's driveway,
Chirp was marching past.
After falling in as ordered,
Chip marched along as last.

Going toward Duke, turning right,
marching toward King,
Chip informed General Chirpenhower
he was ready for studying.

Born in 1929,
Jacqueline Lee Bouvier.
Hired by a D.C. newspaper,
to be an inquiring reporter.

Her father, lawyer and stockbroker,
an eligible New York bachelor.
Her mother from wealth married him,
sixteen years her senior.

Among the many people she met,
Congressman Jack Kennedy.
Married in 1953,
Jack ran for the presidency.

The new First Lady insisted being called
Mrs. Kennedy.
She restored the presidential mansion
following history.

Instead of being a political adviser,
she offered personal advice
and focused on their relationship.
Was viewed by many as nice.

November of 1963,
tragedy impacted the nation.
In Dallas, President Kennedy
was assassinated.

Addressing what it felt like to become a First Lady
of the United States at age 31, Mrs. Kennedy said:
*I feel as though I have just been turned into a
piece of public property. It's really frightening to
lose your anonymity at thirty-one.*

"Mrs. Kennedy was so young
to become First Lady."

"From losing anonymity
to widowed Kennedy."

A week had passed for Chip and Chirp,
both ready to study, indeed.
As usual, Chip started the story,
a matter of routine.

Born in December of 1912,
Claudia Alta Taylor.
Her nickname Lady Bird thought given
by Nurse Alice Tittle.

An entrepreneur and merchandiser,
her father, financially sound.
Her mother, 50 and pregnant, died
after tripping and falling down.

A college graduation present,
her father planned sightseeing.
A friend advised she see a Texan
in Washington, D.C.

She didn't, but they eventually met.
He proposed to her.
Telling him she'd think about it;
they married weeks later.

November 1963,
Johnson, President.
He valued his wife's political opinions,
she, not reticent.

In '64, the First Lady
traveled by train throughout
eight southern states to support
the Civil Rights Act.

An entertaining White House Hostess,
reflected cultural intent.
Many foreign diplomats
attended special events.

Another First Lady Johnson project,
American beautification,
gained national appeal and spread–
visibly throughout the nation.

Mrs. Johnson viewed the role of First Lady *as an unpaid public servant elected by one person–her husband.*

> *"First Lady Johnson, a strong woman, was her husband's adviser."*

> *"She traveled by train throughout the South, a Civil Rights supporter."*

Chirp found their book almost dry,
hoped this tale upbeat.
Since the death of Kennedy,
a cloud hung over D.C.

Born in March of 1912,
Thelma Catherine Ryan.
Her father, a silver miner and farmer;
her mother, a homemaker.

Her mother died; Thelma took charge.
Then changed her name to Pat.
After college, a high school teacher
learning to act.

Participating in amateur theater,
she met Richard Nixon.
They married, working as a team
when making all decisions.

First Lady Nixon welcomed thousands
to the White House, enabling
expanded access for the handicapped,
visually and hearing disabled.

Intellectual, not politically ambitious,
First Lady Nixon focused
on the relationship with her husband–
her giving somewhat unnoticed.

First Lady Pat Nixon said: *The most traditinal
duty of a First Lady is serving as a hostess of
the Executive Mansion, just as she would in her
husband's home. . . . Being First Lady is the
hardest unpaid job in the world.*

"Marriage, teamwork, resignation,
another cloud over the capital."

"The Nixons once a unified team—
how could this have happened?"

Born April of 1918,
Elizabeth Ann Bloomer.
Her father had issues with alcohol;
her mother, domineering.

She took dance lessons as a child,
then worked as a model like Gerry.
Following divorce, she met Ford;
she and the lawyer soon married.

The resignation of Spiro Agnew,
Ford named replacement.
When Nixon resigned as President,
Ford named replacement.

Being White House Hostess allowed
the country to hear
her sharing her honesty publicly—
Time's Woman of the Year.

First Lady Ford admitted discussing
issues with her best friend;
choosing to agree to disagree–
because **he** was President.

Admittedly, she used pillow talk
to share her policy issues.
First Lady Ford used intellect,
promoting her husband's wishes.

First Lady Betty Ford said: *Being ladylike does not
require silence. Why should my husband's job or
yours prevent us from being ourselves? I do not
believe that being First Lady should prevent me
from expressing my ideas.*

> *"Sometimes honest to a fault,
> freely speaking her mind . . ."*

> *". . . Mrs. Ford, opinionated,
> could end up in a bind."*

Chirp arrived early at the church.
Chip flew over and landed.
Since their book was almost dry,
they dragged it single-handed.

Born August 1927,
Evelyn Rosalynn Smith.
Her father operated a garage;
her mother, a seamstress.

Starting college, she had a crush
on her best friend's brother.
Writing during Academy years,
they married in the summer.

When Carter ran for President,
neither he nor she
had seen the interior of the White House
before living free.

President, First Lady, daughter, two sons,
plus the grandchildren
filled the White House upper two floors.
"First Lady" became "Rosalynn."

First Lady Carter hosted hundreds
of suppers with southern fare,
obviously removing formal protocol,
trying to spend with care.

Involved in mental health issues,
named Honorary Chair
of the Commission on Mental Health,
plus equal rights aware.

Serving as the President's adviser,
her intellect and ambition
for political decisions and policies
promoted her husband's positions.

First Lady Rosalynn Carter believed that to be a
successful First Lady, *You have to have confidence
in your ability, and then be tough enough to follow
through.*

> *"First Lady Carter brought changes
> to White House events."*

> *"She moved her family into the mansion,
> and worked with the Cabinet."*

Chirp heard Chip singing nearby,
sounding almost gleeful.
She wondered just how Chip had reached
the top of Trinity's steeple.

Born in 1921,
Anne Frances Robbins.
Her mother, a silent screen actress;
her father, a car dealer.

Mother named her daughter Nancy
before divorce, remarriage.
Adopted when about fourteen,
Davis, the name she carried.

The romantic lead opposite Reagan,
who became President
of the Screen Actors Guild,
married him and reinvented.

Mrs. Reagan's political views
majorly impacted her husband.
She a Conservative; he a Democrat,
becoming a Conservative Republican.

In 1980, Reagan was elected
President with George H.W.
Mrs. Reagan had an image problem
causing her media trouble.

As Hostess, Mrs. Reagan made
dinners political occasions.
The White House needing updating,
she led a renovation.

Given the title "Queen Nancy,"
she chose to help kids know
through her anti-drug campaign,
Just Say No.

Agreed by many historians,
she, Reagan's adviser,
used intellect and ambition
to make her husband wiser.

First Lady Nancy Reagan said: *However the First Lady fits in, she has a unique role to play in looking after her husband. And it's only natural that she'll let him know what she thinks.*

"Mrs. Reagan had significant power over her husband."

"Not particularly liked by some, she had a good drug program."

Chip was ready to hop right in
to starting a new tale.
Chirp drank from the faucet's puddle,
then dipped the tip of her tail.

Born in 1925,
Baby Barbara Pierce.
Her father, an executive at McCall's;
her mother, a state justice's daughter.

During her junior year in school,
she met George and conversed.
Secretly engaged when leaving for college,
she quit to marry him first.

Mother of six, her hair turned white,
unable to leave home
upon the death of her little girl.
Son George didn't leave her alone.

Barbara fell into the routine
of being a traditional wife,
while George increasingly devoted his time
to a successful business life.

George H.W. elected President.
Mrs. Bush then raised
White House entertaining anew,
making guests feel engaged.

Universal literacy
and local charities,
First Lady Bush focused on
Number One Authority.

First Lady Barbara Bush said: *There is no job
description for the First Lady and she's only there
because her husband got elected President.*

"Wife and mother her favorite positions
and promoting literacy, . . ."

". . . Mrs. Bush, a good hostess,
relaxed her company."

Realizing their First Lady tales
would be ending soon,
Chip asked Chirp to make plans
for telling the remaining two.

Leaving, Chip sensed something wrong.
He flew to Saint Mark on the roof
to be alone and ponder about
his nagging burden of proof.

Born in 1947,
Hillary Diane Rodham.
Her father, a college graduate;
her mother, a secretary.

Social responsibility her cause,
active in her youth group,
she attended a college with attitude
for socially active roots.

Feminist movement, civil rights,
and social change affected
her perspective as did Clinton,
the marriage partner selected.

In the election of '92,
Clinton defeated Bush
and Ross Perot, Independent candidate–
something of an ambush.

Mrs. Clinton, White House Hostess,
included culture in events.
Child advocacy, women's interests–
her primary social attempts.

First Lady Clinton used her intellect
to promote her husband's interests
and the nation's without suppressing
her personal interests.

First Lady Hillary Clinton said: *People can judge me
for what I've done. And I think when somebody's
out in the public eye, that's what they do. So I'm
comfortable with who I am, what I stand for, and
what I've always stood for.*

"Concerned about social issues,
Mrs. Clinton studied . . ."

". . . to implement her ideas,
tending to be hurried.

Their last day for First Lady tales
began with a sunny massage.
Chip raced Chirp once again
from rooftop to parking garage.

Born in 1946,
Baby Laura Welch.
Her parents, upper middle class,
pleased with her A's in college.

Following graduation, a trip
with her family.
First working as an insurance clerk,
then leading a school library.

George and she in the same complex,
met at a barbecue.
They planned to see each other again,
announcing marriage soon.

Bush chose running for the presidency,
Mrs. Bush by his exterior.
As White House Hostess, First Lady Bush
used Camp David's interior.

While in the White House, First Lady Bush
worked with literacy.
She made it a point to appear apolitical,
aware of her legacy.

First Lady Laura Bush said: *As seeing herself as
just his wife and she would never do anything to
undermine her husband's point of view. . . . For
a First Lady, there are moments of maximum,
political controversy, and they often strike
without warning.*

"First Lady Bush 43,
worked with literacy."

"The wife of a rising politician,
aware of her legacy."

Pleased with their adventurous days
shared this third summer,
The Two flew to Trinity's rooftop
to consider next summer.

Two dove friends sat silently
atop the church so high.
Simultaneously happy and sad,
Chirp quietly said, "Goodbye."

As she flew above Duke Street,
Chip whispered, "Goodbye,"
watching until his friend Chirp
disappeared into the sky.

Lacking the energy or desire
to leave the roof for home,
he slowly flew to the faucet puddle,
glad they'd finished the tome.

Not feeling himself on Labor Day,
Chip returned to the church,
wanting only to rest alone
behind Holy Trinity Church.

The following summer Chirp arrived,
looking for her friend Chip.
After searching Downtown Lancaster,
she concluded his heart might've quit.

Thankful for the summers they'd shared,
knowing time continues,
she flew to sit with the Newspaper Reader–
her thoughts of Chip continuing.

If one were forced to leave their place,
another'd appear soon.
A male dove quietly landed
beside Chirp on the statue.

BONNIE BARB FRICK

Bonnie Barb Frick is a retired high school English teacher. The keys to unlocking her interest in writing books are her two grandchildren. When writing picture books gave way to writing chapter books, she discovered Chip and Chirp, two imaginary dove friends, as storytellers.

While living in a suburb of Lancaster, the two doves use their talents to meet and share another story of Jesus on another day for the book *Chip and Chirp Tell Stories of Jesus.*

After moving to Lancaster, Chip and Chirp spend one summer visiting and sharing stories about the City in *Birds' Eye Views of Historic Downtown Lancaster* and a second summer sharing stories about twelve modern American Presidents and their First Ladies in *Chip and Chirp Tell Presidential Tales.*

In *History Is for the Birds*, Chip and Chirp are viewed revisiting Lancaster, PA, and Washington, D.C., in verse. Intermittently, they return to interject fowl opinions.

Made in the USA
Columbia, SC
06 September 2018